Writer's Notebook

By the Editors of TIME For Kids

Teacher Created Materials
PUBLISHING

CM 10147 (i1000)

TIME For Kids
Editorial Director: Keith Garton
Editor: Jonathan Rosenbloom
Project Editor: The Quarasan Group, Inc.
Design Production: The Quarasan Group, Inc.
Illustrator: The Quarasan Group, Inc.
Teacher Reviewers: Holly Albrecht, WI; Marian Evans, TX; Ryann Kelso, IL; Karen Lawson, OH; Christine Libeau, CA; Karen Mauro, NY; Julie Morgan, NE; Mary Paskvan, MN; Jeff Reed, PA; Jana Underwood, TX

Teacher Created Materials
Publisher: Rachelle Cracchiolo, M.S. Ed.
Editor-in-Chief: Sharon Coan, M.S. Ed.
Editorial Project Manager: Dona Herweck Rice

ISBN: 0-7439-0147-9

Teacher Created Materials
5301 Oceanus Drive
Huntington Beach, CA 92649-1030
http://www.tcmpub.com

Photography credits:
Page 5: PhotoDisc, Inc.; p. 6: Comstock; p. 8: PhotoDisc, Inc., MetaTools; p. 9: MetaTools; p. 10: MetaTools; p. 11: MetaTools; p. 12: MetaTools; p. 14: PhotoDisc, Inc., MetaCreations/Kai, Corbis; p. 16: PhotoDisc, Inc.; p. 18: PhotoDisc, Inc.; p. 20: PhotoDisc, Inc.; p. 24: PhotoDisc, Inc., MetaCreations/Kai; p. 31: PhotoDisc, Inc.; p. 33: PhotoDisc, Inc.; p. 34: PhotoDisc, Inc.; p. 36: PhotoDisc, Inc.; p. 37: MetaCreations/Kai; p. 38: Comstock; p. 40: MetaCreations/Kai; p. 41: Wildside Press; p. 42: PhotoDisc, Inc.; p. 43: PhotoDisc, Inc.; p. 46: MetaCreations/Kai, PhotoDisc, Inc.; p. 47: PhotoDisc, Inc.; p. 51: PhotoDisc, Inc.; p. 54: PhotoDisc, Inc.; p. 60: Artville; p. 62: Corbis; p. 69: PhotoDisc, Inc., Artville; p. 73: MetaCreations/Kai; p. 80: MetaCreations/Kai, PhotoDisc, Inc.; p. 81: PhotoDisc, Inc.; p. 82: PhotoDisc, Inc.; p. 83: PhotoDisc, Inc.; p. 84: PhotoDisc, Inc.

For more writing practice: www.timeforkids.com/hh/writeideas

Table of Contents

Using Your Writer's Notebook

Do you know the secret to becoming a better writer? Write, and then write some more!

At TIME For Kids, writers go through many of the same challenges that you do as you write. The TFK writers must find a topic, research the facts, get organized, write a draft, revise their writing, and edit and proofread their writing. Think of writing as a process, steps that can help you become a better writer.

Your TIME For Kids Writer's Notebook is a handy tool you can use when you write. In your Notebook you will find

- a guide to the writing process, featuring a section about each of the steps that good writers follow.
- mini-lessons on skills such as writing smooth sentences.
- samples of different kinds of writing, from reports to poetry.
- lists of words that will make your writing clear and interesting.

Remember, have fun with your writing. Find an idea or story that matters to you and makes you want to write. Then get busy and start writing!

Steps in the Writing Process

1

Prewriting—Choose a topic. Then plan and organize what you are going to write about.

Jake, my pet snake

green
shiny black eyes
sticky tongue
likes to flick

2

Drafting—Write your ideas down in a rough draft, or first copy.

I have a pet snake named jake.

He is green and has shiny black eyes.

He also has a sticky tonge. Jake likes

to flick his tongue

Revising—Get other readers' responses through sharing and reflecting. Make changes to improve your draft.

Meet Jake

I have a pet snake named jake. He is emerald green and has shiny black eyes. He also has a long sticky tonge. Jake flicks his tongue to catch food to eat

Editing and Proofreading—Find and fix any mistakes.

Meet Jake

I have a pet snake named jake. He is emerald green and has shiny black eyes. He also has a long sticky ~~tonge.~~ tongue Jake flicks his tongue to catch food to eat⊙

Publishing—Write your final copy and share it with others.

Meet Jake

I have a pet snake named Jake. He is emerald green and has shiny black eyes. He also has long sticky tongue. Jake flicks his tongue to catch food to eat.

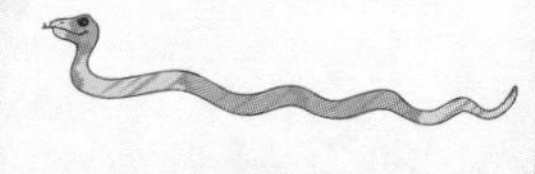

TFK Tips for Writers

You can go back and repeat a step any time during the writing process.

Now let's take a closer look at each step in the writing process.

Prewriting

Prewriting is the time to plan and organize what you are going to write about. One way to do this is to draw a picture of the topic you have chosen and then list words that describe it.

Drafting

Drafting is the time to get your ideas down on paper. Use your notes from the Prewriting activity to write your first draft. Don't worry about mistakes. You can fix those later.

Revising

Revising is the time to think about your writing and share it with others. Get responses from other readers. Use their comments and your own ideas to make changes that will improve your draft. What changes did the writer make to improve the draft on page 9?

Meet Jake

I have a pet snake named jake.

He is emerald green and has shiny

black eyes. He also has a long sticky

tonge. Jake flicks his tongue to catch

food to eat

Editing and Proofreading

Editing and Proofreading is the time to find and fix any mistakes before you make a final copy. Notice how the writer used proofreading marks to show what needed to be fixed.

I have a pet snake named jake. ≡

He is emerald green and has shiny

black eyes. He also has a long sticky

tongue

~~tonge~~. Jake flicks his tongue to catch

food to eat ⊙

Publishing

Publishing is the time to write your final copy and share it with others.

Meet Jake

I have a pet snake named Jake. He is emerald green and has shiny black eyes. He also has long sticky tongue. Jake flicks his tongue to catch food to eat.

1

Prewriting

Time to plan and organize what you are going to write about

Getting Started

Where do writers get ideas? Writers get ideas from the world around them. They write about people they know, places they visit, things they do, and topics that interest them.

Look and Listen!

Writers look and listen. They notice things such as colors, sounds, and smells. Look at these pages from a writer's notebook. How did the writer describe her surroundings?

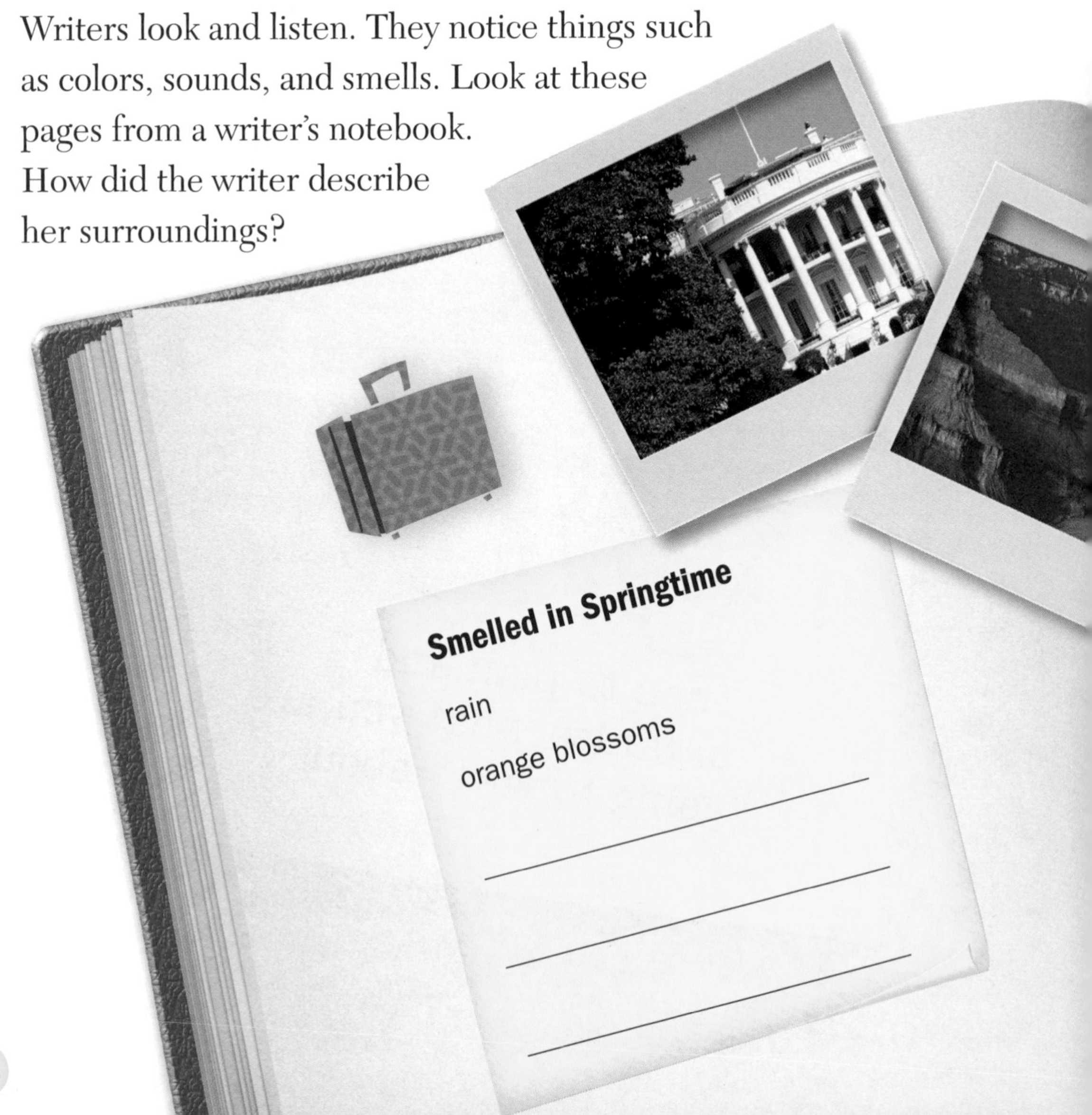

Try This!

Start your own personal writer's notebook. Keep it with you so that you can write anywhere and anytime. Then be aware. Make notes in your notebook about things you see and hear. Warm up by adding to each entry in the writer's notebook below.

Be a List Keeper

Good writers are list keepers, too. Making lists gives them ideas for topics to write about. You can keep your lists in your writer's notebook. How would you complete each list on this page?

Fun Places I Have Visited

1 Wisconsin Dells

2 Disney World

3 Grand Canyon

4 ______________________________

5 ______________________________

Animals I Want to Know More About

1 hamsters

2 lions

3 ______________________________

4 ______________________________

5 ______________________________

Things I Want to Do Someday

1 learn to swim

2 go to space camp

3 go camping

4 ______________________________

5 ______________________________

Try This!

Here are some more lists. How would you complete each? Write your ideas.

Favorite Games

1 basketball

2 hopscotch

3 soccer

4 ____________________

5 ____________________

Top Ten Fun and Fun-to-Say Words

1 tiny

2 swish

3 fussy

4 crash

5 cheese

6 ____________________

7 ____________________

8 ____________________

9 ____________________

10 ____________________

Time to Write

Make your own list. Write a title for the list. Then review your list when you need to find a topic to write about.

Title: ____________________

1 ____________________

2 ____________________

3 ____________________

4 ____________________

5 ____________________

6 ____________________

Choose a Topic

As part of Prewriting, you need to choose a topic to write about. That's when your writer's notebook comes in handy. You can review your notes and choose an idea that would make a good topic.

Narrow It Down

When you write, make sure your topic is not too big. Choose an idea that you can write about easily in one piece of writing. If your topic is too big, you may need to narrow it down, or break it into smaller parts. You can use an idea comb to help you.

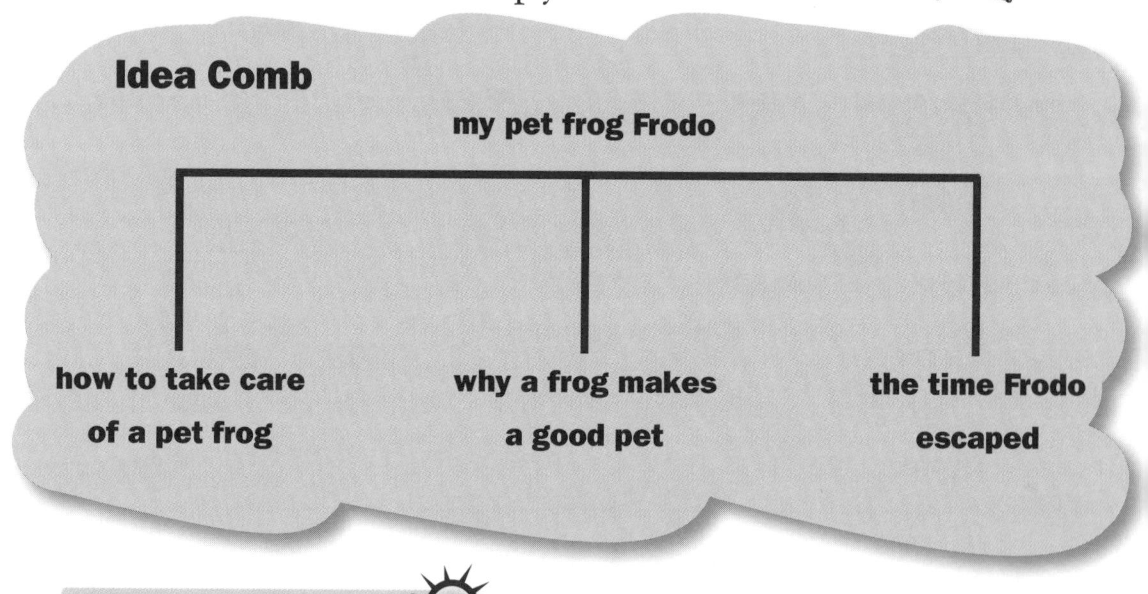

TFK Tips for Writers

Talk about your topic ideas with a partner. Which ideas does your partner like best?

Some topics are too big to write about—there is just too much to say. Using a topic map like the one below is another way to narrow your topic. It will help you choose an idea that you can write about in a story or brief report.

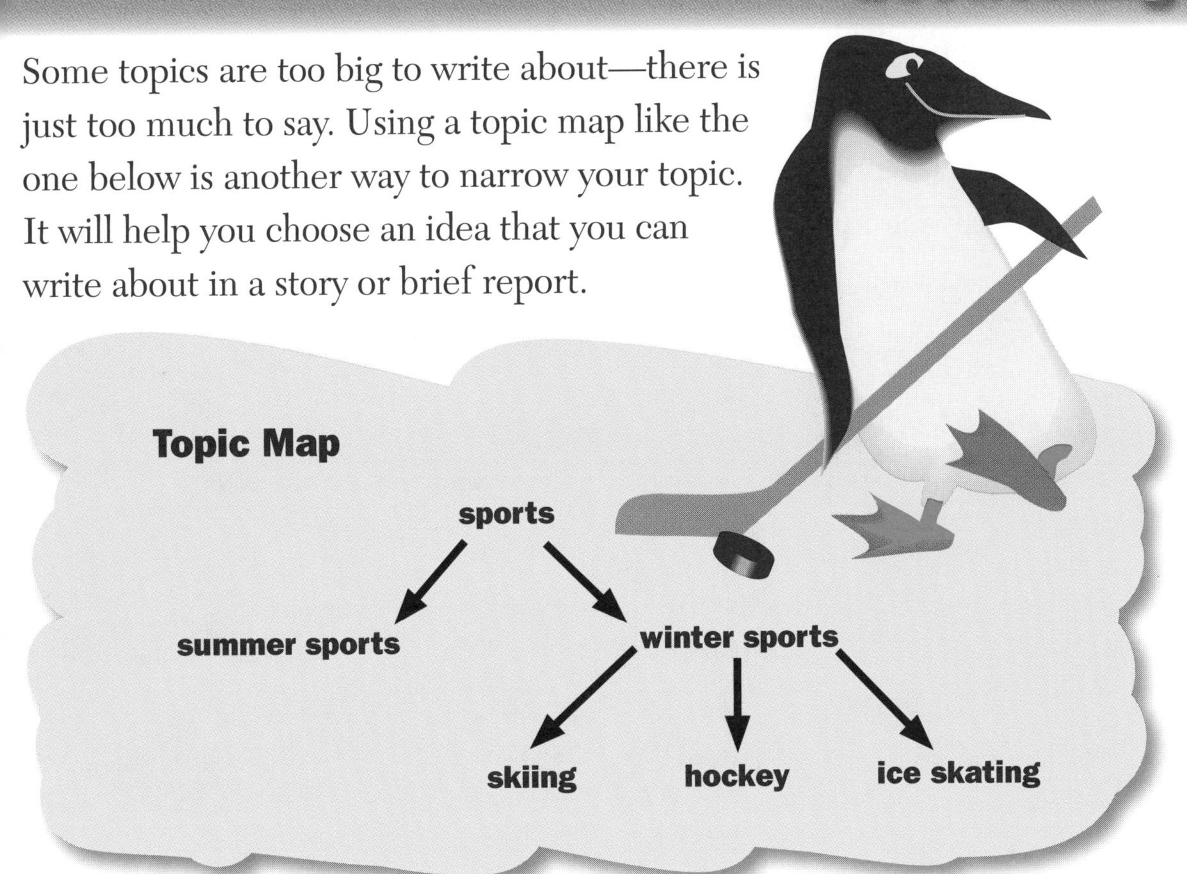

Try This!

Look at a topic you are planning to write about. Is it too big? Use one of the organizers shown here to narrow it down. On a separate sheet of paper, write your big idea. Then write smaller parts of that idea below. Choose one small part to write about.

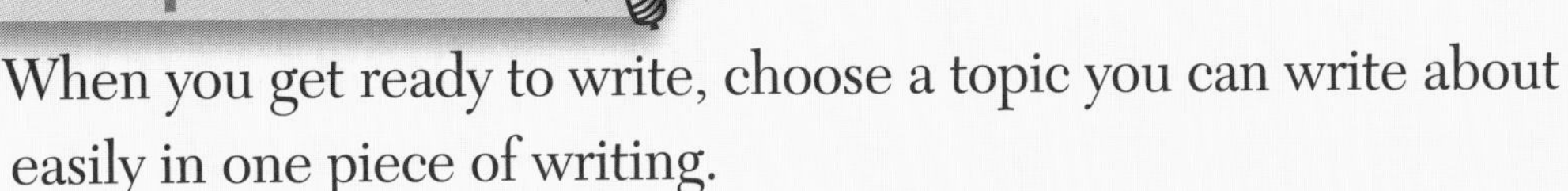

Start Thinking

You've chosen a topic and narrowed it down. Now think about what you want to say and how you will say it. The questions below can help you.

Ask Before You Write	
What am I writing?	Am I writing a fable or a folk tale? a report? a letter?
Who is my audience?	Is it my teacher? my classmates? my parents?
What is my purpose?	Do I want to entertain? to inform or explain? to persuade someone to do something?
Do I have all the facts I need?	If not, where can I look? Will I use an encyclopedia or atlas? Internet sites or nonfiction books?
How will I publish my writing?	Will I publish it on a school Internet site or make a book? Will I read it in class or give a speech? Will I include photographs or illustrations?

Try This!

What are you planning to say about your topic? How are you planning to say it? Before you begin, ask yourself the questions in the chart. Use your answers to help you plan what you want to write.

Organize Your Ideas

Once you have decided what to write about, you need to arrange your ideas in a way that makes sense.

Use a Graphic Organizer

You can use graphic organizers to help you organize your ideas. Here are two examples. You'll find many others on TIME For Kids Homework Helper site: **www.timeforkids.com/hh/writeideas**

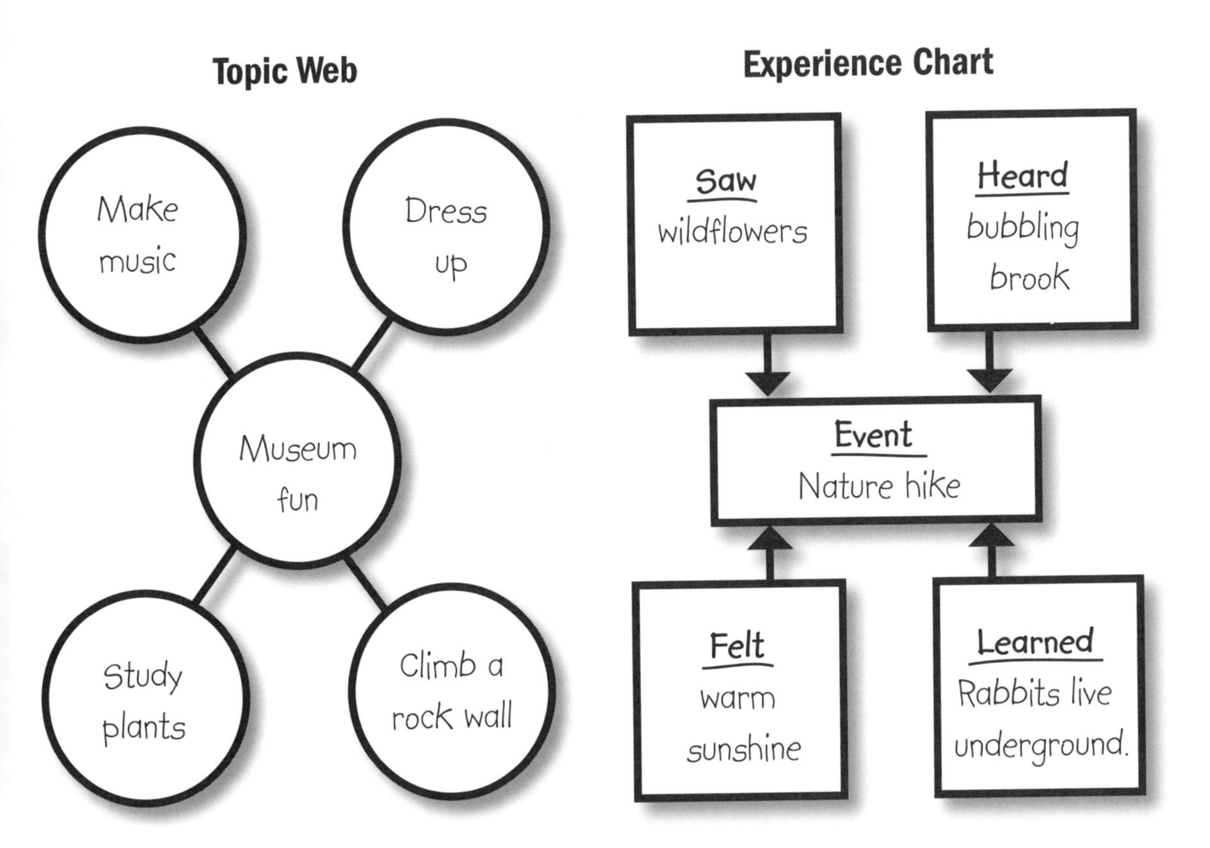

Use a topic web to plan a report, an article, or a biography. An experience chart works well for planning a personal narrative.

More Graphic Organizers

Fiction Story Map	
Beginning	On a rainy morning, Meg is surprised when a gust of wind carries her into the sky.
Middle	Meg has several adventures visiting places around the world, such as the Great Wall of China and the Eiffel Tower, as she tries to make her way home.
Ending	Almost ready to give up on ever seeing her home and family again, a magical seagull carries Meg home.

Use a fiction story map to plan a fable, folk tale, fantasy, or adventure story.

Try This!

Here is a Venn diagram you could use to plan a paper comparing dogs and cats. When you write to compare, you tell what is different and what is the same about each person, animal, or object. How would you complete the diagram?

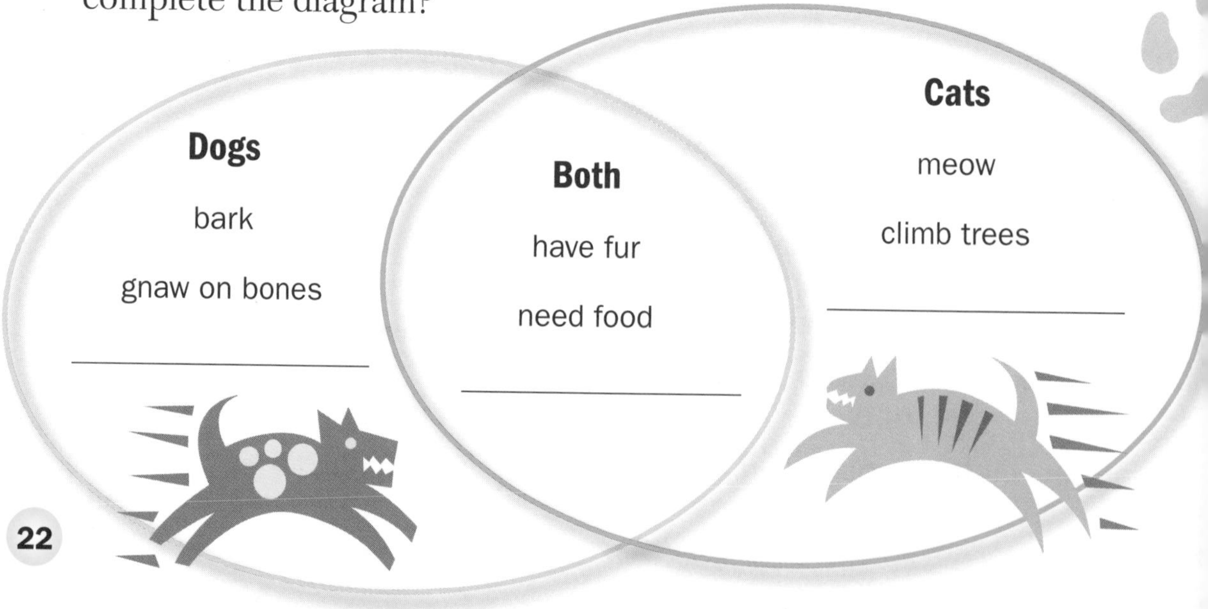

Dogs

bark

gnaw on bones

____

Both

have fur

need food

____

Cats

meow

climb trees

____

2
Drafting
Time to write
a working draft,
or first copy

What Is a First Draft?

A first draft is your first attempt to write something. It is your chance to get all your ideas down on paper.

Tips From a Pro

Read the interview with writer Cindy Crown below. What tips does she give to help you write a first draft?

Interview with a Writer

Q: When you begin to write, what do you do first?

A: First, I think about my ideas and make a plan. I think about what I want to say and how I want to say it. I also think about whom I'm writing for.

Q: What do you do next?

A: Next, I just start to write. I write down all my ideas. I don't worry if my writing doesn't sound right. I write on every other line of my paper so that it's easy to make changes later.

Q: If you are not sure about how to spell a word, what do you do?

A: I usually circle the word. The circle reminds me to check it later in a dictionary.

Q: Why is it important to write a first draft?

A: A first draft gives me a chance to get down all my ideas without having to stop. Then I can check a dictionary or think about the order of my ideas.

A Sample First Draft

Read the excerpt shown below. It is from a first draft of a story about a make-believe character. What did the writer do to show that he or she is not finished writing this part of the story? Do you see other changes that the writer might make?

MeMe

There are many chores that I have to do, but there is one chore that I don't have to do anymore. Guess who has to do that chore now. My imajineree friend does it!

Does this belong here?

Her name is MeMe. She is half cat and half horse, and she has wings. MeMe is two years old. So, she can take me to skool and she will pick me up to go home. I love to ride MeMe everywhere.

What Is Fiction?

Fiction is a kind of writing that has made up characters and events. Narrative fiction includes folk tales, fairy tales, fables, fantasy, and stories about people like you.

Folk Tales and Fairy Tales

Folk tales and **fairy tales** are fiction. These kinds of stories often include pretend characters such as elves and animals that can talk. Folk and fairy tales often begin "Once upon a time." *Stone Soup* is a folk tale. *Hansel and Gretel* is a fairy tale.

Try This!

What folk tale or fairy tale do you know? Write the title below. What makes it a folk or fairy tale?

____

Fables

Fables are fiction. Fables are stories that teach a lesson or moral. They may also have animal characters. The *Tortoise and the Hare* is a fable. So is *The Grasshopper and the Ant.*

Try This!

What fable do you know? Write the title below. What makes it a fable?

Fantasy

Fantasy stories are fiction. Fantasy stories often have magical characters. They may also take place in magical places where anything can happen. *Alice in Wonderland* is a fantasy.

Try This!

What fantasy story do you know? Write the title below. What makes it a fantasy?

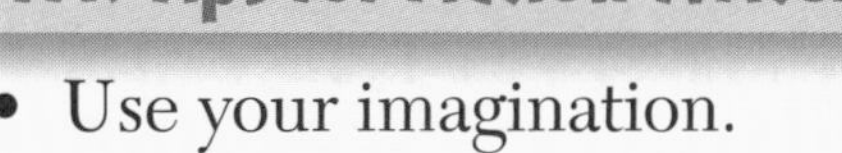

- Use your imagination.
- Tell the story in order.
- Draw pictures.

Time to Write

Look at a fiction story you are writing. Read the tips in the chart. Which tip could you try?

Story Pieces

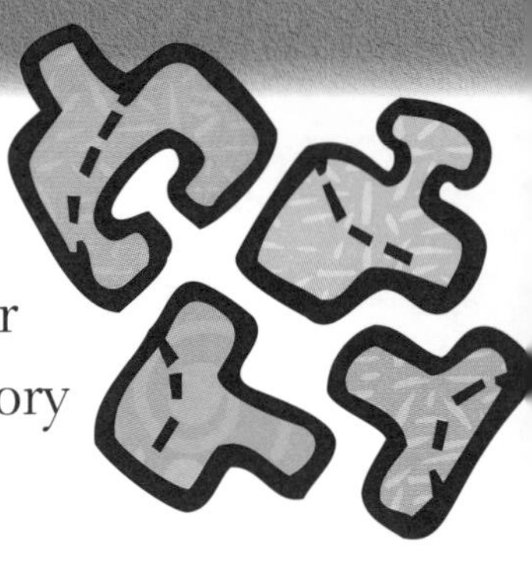

A story is like a puzzle. It has pieces that fit together to make a story picture. The pieces, or parts, of a story are characters, setting, and plot.

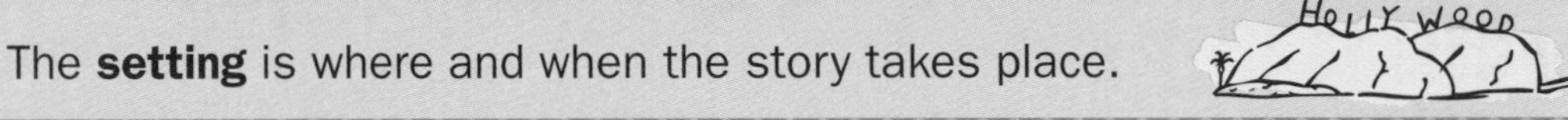

Parts of a Story
• The **characters** are whom the story is about.
• The **setting** is where and when the story takes place.
• The **plot** is what happens in the story. It tells the problem that the characters have and how they solve it.

TFK Tips for Writers

Use an organizer like the Fiction Story Map on page 22 to plan and draft your story. Be sure to write the events in the order they happened.

Time to Write

Look at a story you are writing. Does it tell who the characters are and what the setting is? Does it tell what the characters' problem is and how they solve it? If not, add the missing story pieces.

Creating Characters

Good writers use details to describe story characters. The chart below shows details that can help make characters seem real.

Character Details
• **How a character looks** Is the character a person, an animal, or a fanciful elf or giant? Does he or she have horns or pink hair? wear green, pointed shoes or an oversized red sweater?
• **How the character acts or feels** Is the character silly? curious? shy?
• **What the character does or likes to do** Does the character like to help people? Does he or she fly? travel back in time?

TFK Tips for Writers

Including dialogue, the speakers' exact words, can bring your characters to life.

Time to Write

Look at a character from a story you are writing. Add details to describe the character more clearly and make the character seem more real.

MeMe Is Back!

On page 25, you read part of a draft about MeMe. Here is another way the writer might have written a part of that draft. Look at how the writer describes MeMe in this draft.

looks

does

feels

My imaginary friend's name is MeMe. MeMe is two years old. She is half cat and half horse and has two wings. The cat half is red, and the horse half is white. The wings are blue. MeMe likes to take me to and from school. We fly fast. One day, MeMe's wings fell off. MeMe needed to find a way to fix them. MeMe was sad. She asked me to help.

Time to Write

Look at a story you are writing. Then look at the checklist below. Ask yourself each question. Add details to your story so that you can answer yes to each question.

TFK Tips for Writers

Use paragraphs to organize your writing. All the sentences in a paragraph are about one main idea.

Checklist for a Story

- ☐ Did I give my story a title?
- ☐ Did I tell where and when my story takes place?
- ☐ Did I tell how the characters look and act? Did I tell what the characters do or like to do?
- ☐ Did I include a problem for my characters to solve?
- ☐ Did I tell how the character or characters solved the problem?
- ☐ Did I tell the story events in order?

What Is Nonfiction?

Nonfiction is a kind of writing that tells about real people and real events. Narrative nonfiction includes true stories about you, or personal narratives. It also includes true stories about other people, or biographies. News stories, reports, and reviews are also nonfiction.

Personal Narrative

A **personal narrative** tells a story about something that happened to you. Read this paragraph from the personal narrative below.

A Day at the Toy Store

Mom picked me up after school. She smiled and said, "We're having Bring Your Son to Work Day at the store next Friday. Would you like to come?" Would I? You bet! Mom works in a big toy store.

TFK Tips for Writers

When you write, write in a way that sounds like you. Let readers hear what you are like and how you feel. **In other words, let them hear your voice!**

Written Report

A **report** gives facts about a topic. Writers find facts in different books and resources. They use these to write their report. Writers may also include charts, graphs, maps, diagrams, and photographs to help readers better understand their report. Look at the example below from a report about rabbits.

A rabbit's sharp senses help keep it safe from harm. Its long ears perk up at the faintest sound. A rabbit's eyes can see in all directions. This allows it to escape from hungry enemies. Even its twitching nose can sense when danger is near.

TFK Tips for Nonfiction Writers

- Write about real people, real animals, and real events.
- Check your facts.
- Use photographs, charts, or other visuals.

Time to Write

Look at a personal narrative, report, or other piece of nonfiction that you are writing. Which tip could you try?

Finding Information

Good writers locate information and check their facts before they write. They find information in resources such as dictionaries, encyclopedias, and nonfiction books. They may also use an atlas or the Internet. What resources do you know?

TFK Tips for Writers

Take good notes on the information you find. Use index cards or a note pad.

Encyclopedia Britannica Online

Sunflower
-looks like giant daisy
-name comes from way its head
turns to follow sun
-food for birds and people
-used in soaps, paints, and chicken feed

Identifying Main Ideas and Supporting Details

When you write a report, each paragraph should have a **main idea.** Write a **topic sentence** for each paragraph that tells the main idea. Then add sentences with **supporting details** that tell more about the main idea. Read the paragraph below from a report on the Red Cross. Notice its order, or organization.

The Red Cross is a group that helps people in times of trouble. Helpers rushed to bring food and water to people in Southeast Asia. Huge waves called tsunami caused floods in several countries there. The Red Cross sent tents, because the water had destroyed the homes of many families. Workers delivered medicine to keep away sickness. The Red Cross helps people around the world.

← Topic sentence

← Supporting detail sentences

Fact or Opinion?

When you write a report, it is important to present facts. You want to give your readers information that is correct.

What Are Facts?

Facts are bits of information that can be proved. You can prove a fact by looking, listening, or doing. You can also check in a trusted resource such as a good encyclopedia.

Fact: Most cats live 10 to 15 years.

What Are Opinions?

Opinions are beliefs that someone has. They tell how a person thinks or feels about certain topics. Words such as *I think*, *I feel*, *easy*, *good*, and *worst* are often used to state opinions.

Opinion: I think cats make the best pets.

Try This!

Read each statement below. Write F if you think the statement is a fact. Write O if you think it is opinion. How could you check your answers?

Fact or Opinion?

_____ All spiders have eight legs.

_____ Orb weaver spiders make the best webs.

_____ I think bats are ugly.

_____ Bats sleep hanging upside down.

Time to Write

Look at a report or other piece of nonfiction that you are writing. Underline the facts. Check them in a resource you trust.

TFK Tips for Writers

Nonfiction writing such as reports and news stories should be based on facts. Check your facts before you write.

I think summer is fun.
There are seven continents.
Green is a pretty color.
There are 365 days in a year.

Writing a News Story

A news story gives important facts about a person, place, object, event, or idea. A news story has a headline that tells what the story is about. News stories often explain or give new information, telling readers something that they do not yet know.

A reporter often plans a news story around the **5 Ws and H.** This way, the reporter will be able to give readers all the important facts. Ask yourself these questions when you write a news story.

The 5 Ws and H of a News Story

- **WHO** or **WHAT** is the story about?
- **WHAT** happened?
- **WHERE** did the event take place?
- **WHEN** did the event take place?
- **HOW** did the event happen?
- **WHY** is this event important?

Try This!

Read this paragraph from the news story below. Phrases that tell **When** and **How** have been labeled. Write **Who, What, Where,** or **Why** in the other boxes.

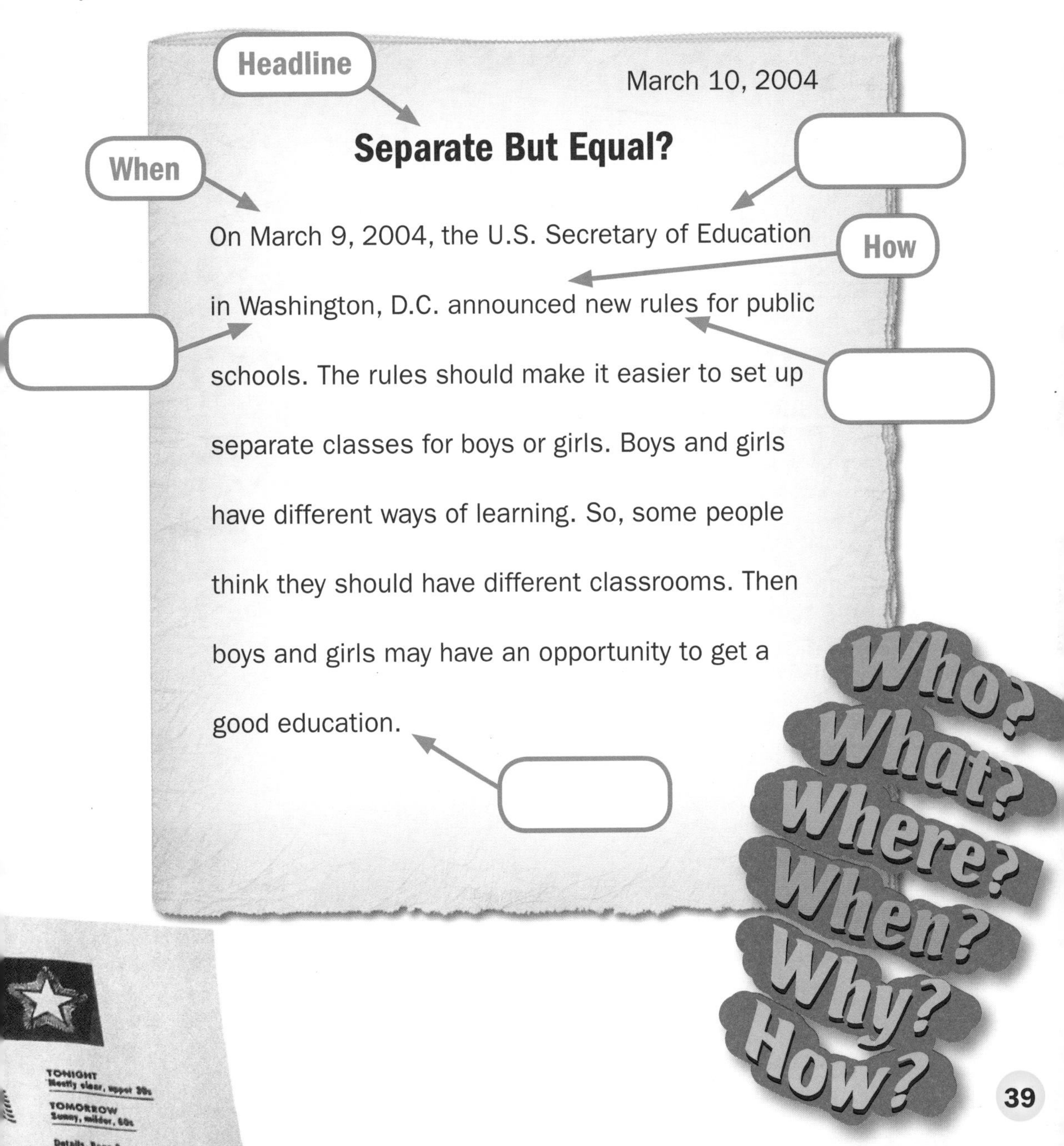

March 10, 2004

Separate But Equal?

On March 9, 2004, the U.S. Secretary of Education in Washington, D.C. announced new rules for public schools. The rules should make it easier to set up separate classes for boys or girls. Boys and girls have different ways of learning. So, some people think they should have different classrooms. Then boys and girls may have an opportunity to get a good education.

Headlines

The title of a news story is called a **headline.** It gives a clue about the topic of the story. It should grab a reader's attention.

TFK Tips for Writers

When you write a news story, include a headline that gets your reader's attention.

Time to Write

Look at a news story that you are writing. Check to see that you've included a headline and the 5 Ws and H. Use the questions on page 38 to help you.

Writing a Biography

A **biography** tells the story of someone's life or about an important event in that person's life. When you write a biography, use the 5 Ws and H to help you organize your writing.

The 5 Ws and H of a Biography

- WHO is the biography about?
- WHAT did the person do?
- WHERE did the person do it?
- WHEN did the person do it?
- HOW did the person do it?
- WHY is the person important?

TFK Tips for Writers

- Choose just one event to write about.
- Use words such as **he, she, his,** and **hers.**
- Use past tense verbs if the person lived long ago.

Research Your Topic

When you write a biography, begin by gathering information about your subject. Encyclopedias, nonfiction books, and the Internet are sources you might use. If the person is still living, you may want to conduct an interview.

The following paragraph is about Harriet Tubman. It describes a cause that was very important to her—helping slaves gain freedom. Notice how the writer has organized the information to tell Harriet's story.

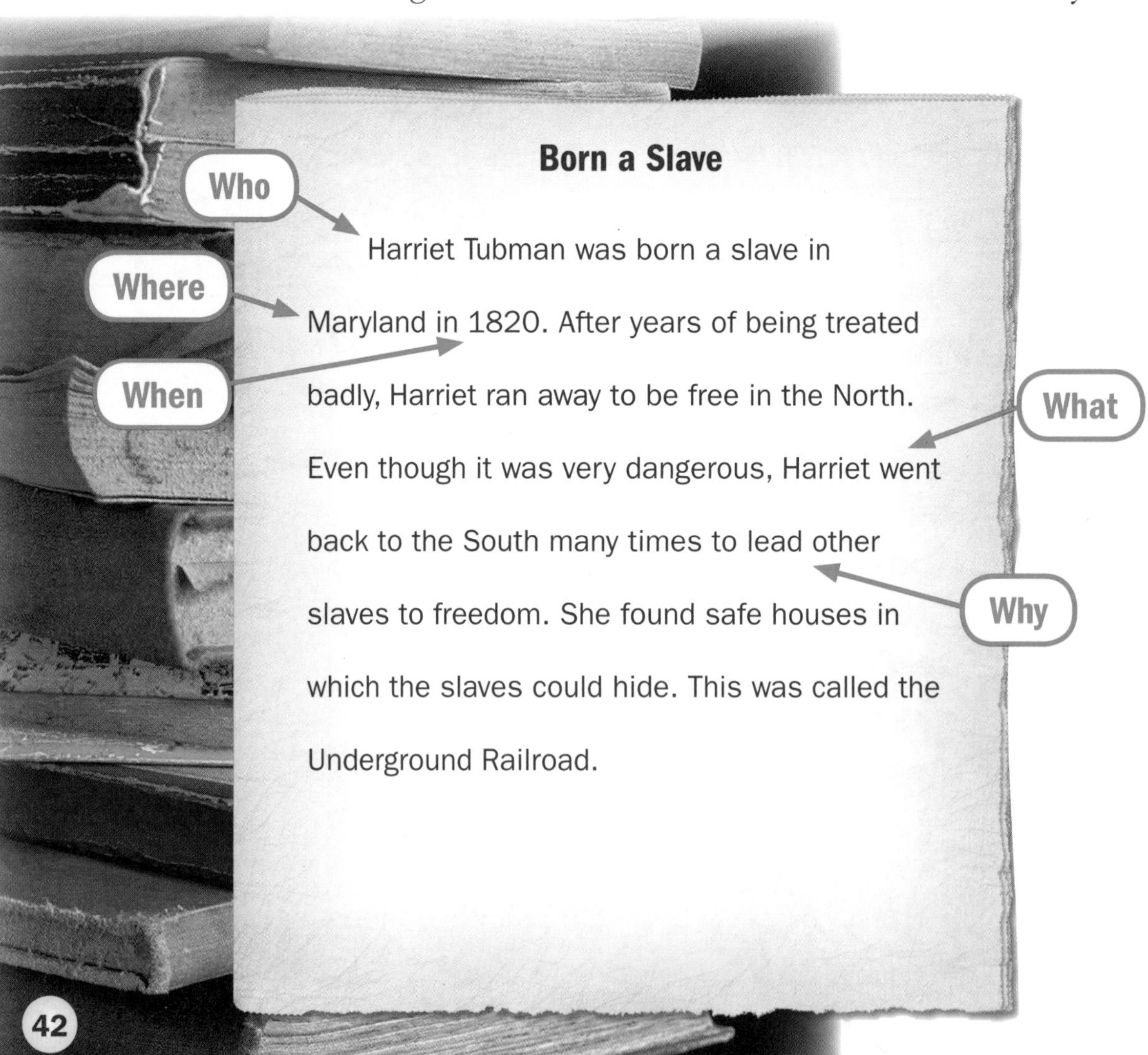

Born a Slave

Harriet Tubman was born a slave in Maryland in 1820. After years of being treated badly, Harriet ran away to be free in the North. Even though it was very dangerous, Harriet went back to the South many times to lead other slaves to freedom. She found safe houses in which the slaves could hide. This was called the Underground Railroad.

Try This!

The paragraph below is from a biography of Thomas Edison. Read it. Which of the 5W and H questions are answered in this paragraph? Which do you think will be answered in the rest of the biography?

Chapter 1

Let There Be Light

It was New Year's Eve, 1879. An inventor named Thomas Alva Edison was about to do something that had never been done before. On that December night, he was going to introduce the world to a new kind of light.

Time to Write

Look at a biography you are writing. Did you include the 5 Ws and H?

Writing to Persuade

When you write to **persuade,** your purpose is to get someone else to think or act a certain way. Depending on your audience, you might write a letter, a speech, or a review.

Start by choosing a topic you really care about. State your opinion or tell readers what you want them to do. Give reasons why you think that way. Be sure to include facts and examples that support your reasons. At the end, state what you want others to do and summarize the reasons why.

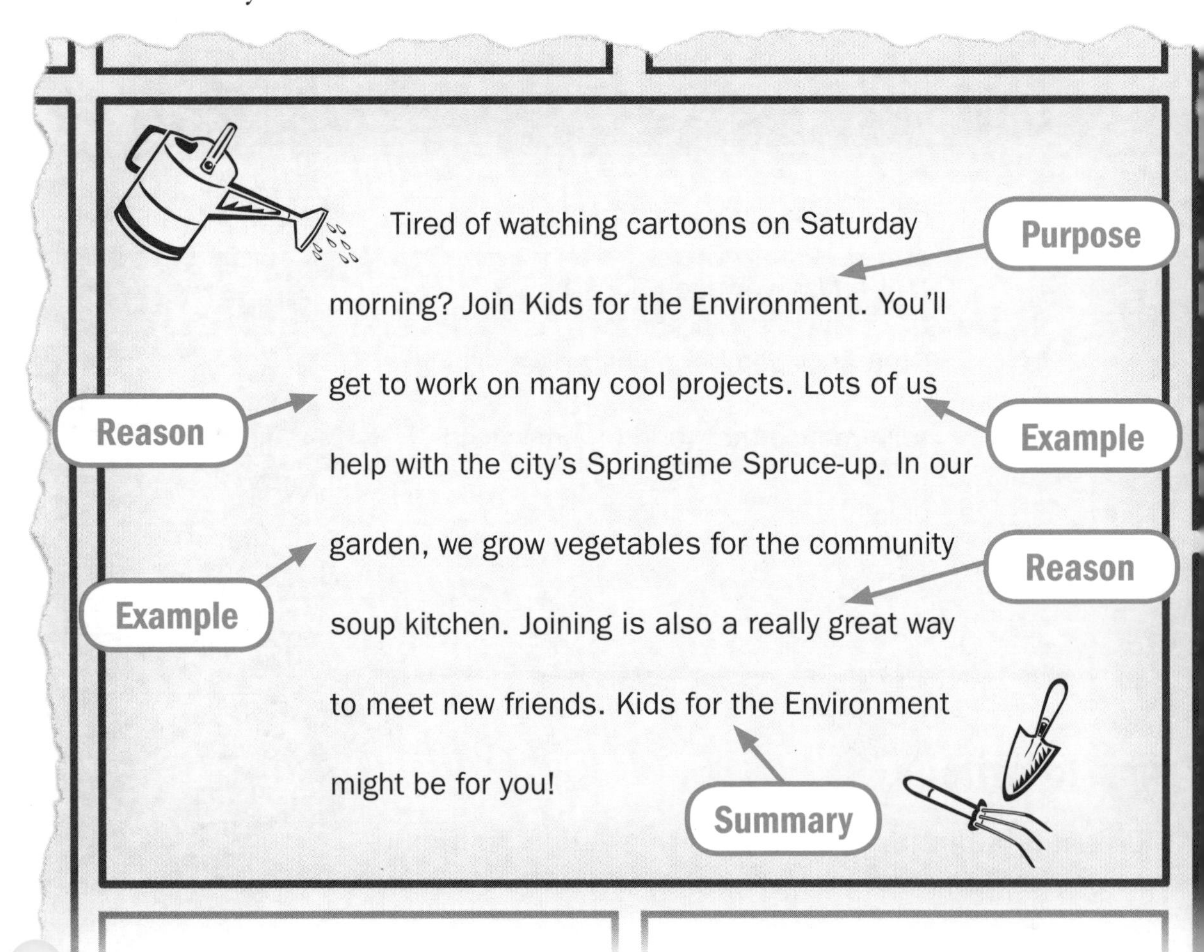

Strong Reasons

Good writers support their opinions with strong reasons. Compare the weak and strong reasons below. Why are the strong reasons better than the weak ones?

OPINION: Kids should not wear hats in school.	
WEAK REASONS	STRONG REASONS
• Hats look silly. • Hats are ugly.	• Hats block other people's view. • Kids play with their hats and make trouble in class.

Try This!

What is your opinion about students wearing in-line skates in school? Write it below. Then write two reasons to support your opinion.

OPINION: ______________________________

REASON 1: ______________________________

REASON 2: ______________________________

TFK Tips for Writers

Write with a positive voice. Tell how taking a certain action will bring good results.

Facts and Examples

Read the letter below. What does the writer think people should do? Find one fact and one example the writer uses to support her opinion. What is the suggestion the writer makes?

Dear Editor,

I think that the town council should make a law to keep dogs out of parks. Dogs bark and chase people. Yesterday, a big dog almost bit me. Keep dogs out of the parks!

Emily James

Try This!

Now it's your turn. What is your opinion about dogs in the parks? Write it here. Then give one fact and one example you could use to support your opinion. Finally, suggest what the reader should do.

OPINION: ______________________________

FACT: ______________________________

EXAMPLE: ______________________________

SUGGESTION: ______________________________

TFK Tips for Writers

- Choose a topic you care about.
- Make sure you have enough reasons to support your opinion about the topic.
- Include facts and examples to support your reasons.

Time to Write

Look at a letter, editorial, or review that you are writing. Then look at the checklist below. Ask yourself each question on the list.

Our town should have a doggy park. Dogs need a place to run and play.

Checklist for Writing to Persuade

- [ ] Did I state my purpose clearly?
- [ ] Did I include at least two strong reasons to support my opinion?
- [ ] Did I include facts and details that explain each reason?
- [ ] Did I make clear what I would like the reader to do?

Strong Openings and Closings

Strong Openings

When you write about an opinion, begin with a **strong opening** sentence or paragraph. A strong opening gives a hint about what your topic will be. The opening should get your audience interested right away.

Weak Opening

I like to play video games. There are many reasons I like to play them.

Strong Opening

I race to the computer. I pick up the control and hold it tightly in my hand. CLICK, CLICK. The adventure begins.

Try This!

Why is the strong opening better than the weak opening? Which words got your attention?

Strong Closings

When you write about an opinion, end with a **strong closing.** A strong closing sums up the important points.

Weak Closing

Now I've told you why I like video games.

Strong Closing

I like to play video games because they make me think and keep me alert. They also help my eyes and hands work together better.

Try This!

Why is the strong closing better than the weak closing? What are the writer's important points?

Time to Write

Look at an opinion you are writing about. Look at your opening. Is each weak or strong? Look at your closing. Does it sum up your main points?

TIME FOR KIDS TO WRITE POETRY

A poem is a special kind of writing. A poem is like a song—it has *rhythm.* Some poems rhyme, and some repeat sounds. Other poems make comparisons. Still others follow a pattern.

These are all tools you can use when you want to write a poem.

See, see! What shall I see?
A horse's head
Where its tail should be!

Play with Sounds

You can use "sound words" to add special effects to your poems. You can also add rhyme.

sound word

SLURP!
A sip from a drink that is cool.
SPLASH!
A belly-flop in my pool.
AHHHH!
Summer and there is no school!

words that rhyme

Time to Write

Write a sound word for

1 rain on a metal roof

____

2 wind on a stormy night

____

3 footsteps on the stairs

____

Say That Again!

Repeating sounds will make any poem more interesting. Try saying this poem out loud—fast!

Betty Botter bought some butter,
But she said, "The butter's bitter";
But a bit of better butter
Will make my batter better.

Time to Write

Dashing dinosaurs danced during dinner.

How would you complete these tongue twisters?

1 Two t__________ t__________ traveled to t__________ .

2 Fran found f__________ f__________ for F__________ .

3 Write your own tongue twister for someone to say: ____________________

____ .

Make Comparisons

In a poem, you can describe things you know in a new way by making comparisons.

A **simile** compares two things using **like** or **as.**

The sun shines like a new penny.
The sun feels as hot as fire.

A **metaphor** tells what something is.

The snow was a white blanket covering the hills.

Try This!

Read each comparison below. Write S if it is a simile. Write M if it is a metaphor.

_____ The stars were sparkling diamonds in the sky.

_____ Tina was as happy as an ant at a picnic.

Word Poems

A word poem follows a letter pattern. Look at the poems below. What letter pattern do you see in each poem?

Stars

Specks of
Twinkling lights
Always there
Ready to brighten the
Sky each night.

Carla

Caring
Artist
Redhead
Lively
Active

Try This!

Write a word poem like those on this page. Use each letter in your name or another word to begin a line of your word poem. Write the title at the top.

3

Revising

Time to make changes to improve your draft

Can I Make My Writing Better?

Good writers think about what they have written. They listen to how their writing sounds and try to make it better. Reading your writing aloud to a partner is often helpful. The listener can tell which parts he or she likes and explain why. Your partner might also point out a part that is not clear and give suggestions for making changes.

Write Smooth Sentences

Joining short, choppy sentences into one longer sentence can make your writing better.

First Draft	Carlos is a great friend! Carlos is kind. Carlos is friendly. Carlos is cheerful.
Revised	Carlos is a great friend! Carlos is kind, friendly, and cheerful.

Time to Revise

To help you revise what you have written, ask yourself these questions:

Is my writing clear?

Do my sentences make sense?

Will my audience be interested?

TFK Tips for Writers

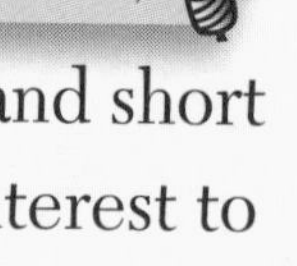

Include both long and short sentences to add interest to your writing.

Is the Title Interesting?

A good title sparks your readers' interest. It gives a hint about your topic and makes your audience want to read on.

Try This!

Read the titles below. What do you think each story is probably about? Which stories would you want to read? Think about why you would be interested.

My Most Terrible Day

Tracks in the Wild

Mama Rocks, Papa Sings

The Secret Path

Time to Revise

Look at something you are writing. Give it a title that tells about the main idea and creates interest for your readers. Warm up by writing a title for a story about each of the following topics.

1 your favorite sport ____________________

2 a pet kitten or puppy ____________________

3 a fun place you have visited ____________________

4 a great invention ____________________

Is the Beginning Strong?

Begin with a sentence that grabs your readers' attention. Starting with a question or a surprise will make your audience want to read more.

Weak Beginning	It snowed last night.
Strong Beginning	When I looked out the window, I knew that this would be a great day.

Write a Catchy Opening

Try these strong beginnings.

Begin with a **question.**	Have you ever wondered how snowflakes form?
Begin with a **quotation.**	"That's just about the weirdest thing I've ever seen!" Rick cried.
Begin with a **description.**	Three tiny balls of fur nuzzled against my cat Franny.

Try This!

Rewrite these weak openings. Write strong sentences that will capture a reader's interest.

1 I heard a squeaking sound in the kitchen.

____

2 My dog can do tricks.

____

Great Beginnings in Books

Read the beginning of *Charlotte's Web.* What is happening? Does it make you want to read more? Why or why not?

"Where's Papa going with that ax?" said Fern to her mother as they were setting the table for breakfast.

"Out to the hog house," replied Mrs. Arable. "Some pigs were born last night."

Time to Revise

Look at something you are revising. Does it have a strong beginning that will make readers want to keep reading? How can you make your opening sentence better?

Are the Sentences In Order?

When you write, organize the ideas or events so your meaning is clear. Put sentences in an order that makes sense to readers.

Try This!

Read the sets of sentences below. Number them to show the beginning, middle, and end of the story. Then read the sentences in order to tell the story.

_______ "Let's take a look," Mrs. Morton said as she carefully examined Fluffy's leg. Gently she removed a thorn and bandaged the kitten's paw.

_______ I can tell that Fluffy's paw is better now. My kitten is just as frisky as ever.

_______ Mrs. Morton knows more about animals than just about anyone it town. When my kitten limped over to its bed and lay down, I knew just where we needed to go.

Time Order Words

One way to organize your writing is by using time order clues. Words such as *first, next, then,* and *finally* can help readers understand how events take place.

Try This!

Read the paragraph below. Find the sentence that is out of order and show where you would move it. Then add time order words to show the order in which the events happen.

Backyard Fun

Every spring, Dad and I plant a garden. __________, small green sprouts pop out of the ground. __________, we prepare the soil. __________, we plant the seeds in rows. __________, we water the garden every day. Soon we'll have peppers, carrots, and beans.

TFK Tips for Writers

When you revise, number your sentences to tell how the events happened. Move any sentences that are not in correct order.

Time to Revise

Read over something that you have written. Would your writing make more sense if you changed the order of some sentences? Are there places where adding time order words would make the meaning clearer?

Is the Meaning Clear?

Sometimes changing the order of words in a sentence can change the meaning. Read both sentences below. How does moving the word *after* change the meaning? Which sentence makes more sense?

The boys pitched their tent **after** they arrived at camp.

After the boys pitched their tent, they arrived at camp.

Try This!

Change the order of some words so the sentences make sense. Read the revised sentences.

1 Dad painted the lawn and mowed the fence.

2 Andy watched TV after he went to sleep.

Adding Details

Adding details will make your writing more interesting. Notice how details add meaning to the sentence below.

- The skaters glided.
- The **graceful** skaters glided **across the frozen lake**.

TFK Tips for Writers

Adding details to your sentences will help readers picture what is happening.

Did You Choose Strong Nouns?

Nouns are words that name persons, places, animals, and things. Good writers choose strong, **exact nouns** to make their writing clear and interesting. Look at the nouns in each sentence below. See how exact nouns give the reader more information.

First Draft	The **men** keep their **things** in the **building**.
Revised	The **firefighters** keep their **raincoats** and **helmets** in the **station house**.

Time to Revise

Replace the nouns in bold type with strong nouns that will make the sentences more exact and interesting. Read aloud your revised sentences.

My class visited a **place** in the country. A **man** showed us fields where he grows **vegetables**. Then we went into a **building** and saw some **animals**.

Try This!

Add to each list of exact nouns.

Persons

1. dentist
2. Grandma
3. ______________
4. ______________

Buildings

1. skyscraper
2. barn
3. ______________
4. ______________

Things or Animals

1. carrot
2. horse
3. ______________
4. ______________

Did You Use Vivid Verbs?

Verbs are words that tell the action in a sentence. When you write, choose **vivid verbs** that will help your reader picture exactly what is happening.

First Draft	The car **went** northward as hailstones **hit** off the hood. Maria and I looked back at the black sky. Maria **said**, "It's a tornado!"
Revised	The car **sped** northward as hailstones **bounced** off the hood. Maria and I looked back at the black sky. Maria **screamed**, "It's a tornado!"

Try This!

Study this list of vivid verbs. Then add interesting verbs that you might use in your writing.

Some Great Verbs

1 gazed
2 gripped
3 bumped
4 flashed
5 bounced

My Favorite Verbs

____

____

____

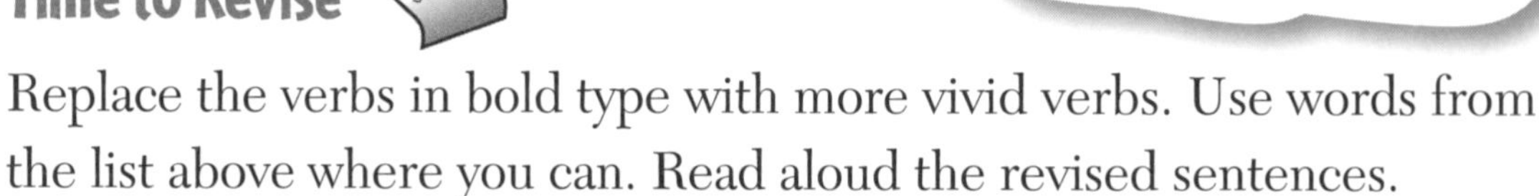

Time to Revise

Replace the verbs in bold type with more vivid verbs. Use words from the list above where you can. Read aloud the revised sentences.

I **looked** out the window. Just then, a bolt of lightening **came** near the plane. I **held** the arm of the seat and closed my eyes. The plane **landed** on the runway. What a ride that was!

Do You Need an Adjective?

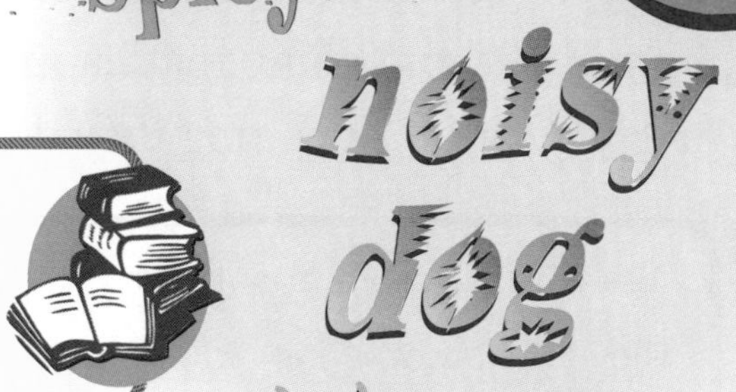

Writers use **adjectives** to describe what they are writing about.

Adjectives describe nouns. They tell how someone or something looks, feels, sounds, smells, and tastes.

Try This!

Look at the sentences below. Notice the adjectives in red. How do they help you picture what the writer is writing about? Now reread the sentences without the words in red. Which group of sentences tells you more?

Liz received a **gorgeous** necklace as a gift. It sparkled with **enormous** blue beads. The color matched her **bright** blue eyes.

Time to Revise

Look at something you are writing. Add adjectives to make your writing more interesting. Warm up by adding adjectives to describe each item at the right.

1 ____________________ cat

2 ____________________ movie

3 ____________________ beach

4 ____________________ sky

5 ____________________ apple

happy noisy lovely tiny narrow gigantic fast speckled lacy careful poor simple skillful young silly kind weak spicy chubby early sharp lucky chilly curly

Do You Need an Adverb?

Good writers use **adverbs** to tell more about something that happens in a story or other writing they do.

will finish tomorrow
snored loudly
played outdoor

Adverbs tell more about verbs. They tell how, when, or where an action takes place.

Try This!

Look at the sentences below. Notice the adverbs in red. How does each one tell about the action? Hint: Look for the verb.

Rick plays **inside** on rainy days. **Yesterday** he built a model racecar. He **quickly** glued the pieces together. **Then** he **carefully** painted the entire car.

Time to Revise

Look at something you have written. Add adverbs to make your writing more interesting. Warm up by adding adverbs to tell how, when, or where about each verb at the right.

1 spoke ______________________________

2 skipped ______________________________

3 answered ______________________________

4 worked ______________________________

5 sang ______________________________

4
Editing and Proofreading
Time to find and fix any mistakes

Writing Great Sentences

Sentences are the building blocks for good writing. A **sentence** is a group of words that tells a complete thought.

Parts of a Sentence

A sentence has two main parts—a **subject part** and a **predicate part.** The **subject** tells whom or what the sentence is about. A subject has a noun. The **predicate** tells what the subject does or is. A predicate has a verb. Look at these examples. Name the noun in each subject and the verb in each predicate.

Subject	Predicate
Two boys	ran in the park.
Ellen	rode her bike.

Time to Edit

Look back at a piece of writing you want to edit. Does each sentence have a subject and a predicate? If not, add the missing sentence part. Practice here by adding a subject or a predicate part to make each sentence below complete.

- A small brown squirrel ____________________
- ____________________ chased after a butterfly.

A Sentence for Every Reason

When you write, make sure you write the different kinds of sentences correctly. Knowing about each kind of sentence will help you do that.

Kinds of Sentences

- A sentence that tells something is a **statement.** It always ends with a period.

  My teacher is Ms Chavez.

- A sentence that asks something is a **question.** It always ends with a question mark.

  Who is Ms Chavez?

- A sentence that expresses strong feeling, such as surprise, fear, or excitement, is an **exclamation.** It ends with an exclamation point.

  You'll never guess what Ms Chavez saw!

- A sentence that asks or tells someone to do something is a **command.** It ends with a period.

  Tell me what Ms Chavez saw.

TFK Tips for Writers

- Begin a sentence with a capital letter.
- End a sentence with the correct punctuation mark.

Try This!

Add the correct punctuation mark to each sentence in the paragraph below.

Are you tired of puzzling over the answer to a problem Sleep on it A study done in 2004 shows why a good night's sleep is important German scientists found that people who sleep at least eight hours a night are better at solving problems Good night

TFK Tips for Writers

Read aloud the paragraph above. Listen to the way your voice changes when you read sentences with different kinds of punctuation.

Time to Edit

Read aloud a piece of writing that you are editing. Does the punctuation mark at the end of each sentence match the sound of your voice as you read?

Writing a Paragraph

Paragraphs organize your writing. A **paragraph** is a group of sentences linked together by a main idea.

Parts of a Paragraph

When you write a paragraph, include a **topic sentence** that tells the topic and main idea. Then add **detail sentences** that support the main idea. End with a **closing sentence** that makes your paragraph sound and feel complete.

Fun in the City

There are many things tourists can do in New York City. They can visit tall buildings, such as the Empire State Building. They can stroll through the city's many different neighborhoods and parks. They can find food from around the world. Tourists will run out of time before they run out of things to do in this great city.

Topic sentence

Supporting detail sentences

Closing sentence

Try This!

Read the paragraph below. Then choose the topic sentence that best tells its main idea. Write the topic sentence on the lines at the beginning of the paragraph.

____

____

The burning sun rose higher over the city. People leaned out of windows and fanned themselves. Children sat limply on curbs. Ice cream and cold drink sellers were the only people working. Even my dog iPod was too hot to bark!

__ It was a beautiful day in January.

__ Nothing beats the excitement of city life!

__ How much longer could the heat wave last?

TFK Tips for Writers

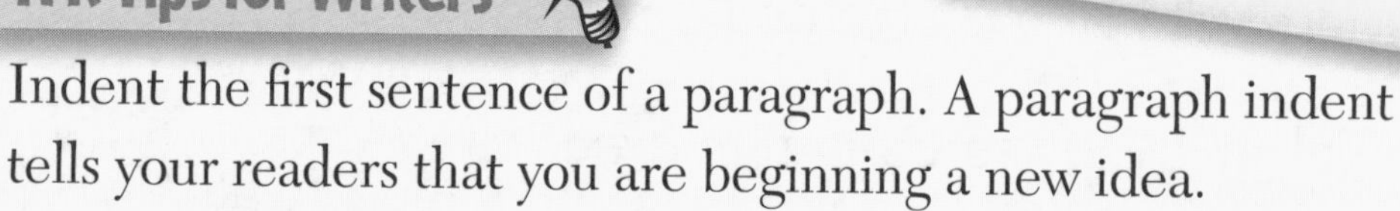

Indent the first sentence of a paragraph. A paragraph indent tells your readers that you are beginning a new idea.

A Strong Finish

The closing sentence should make your paragraph sound and feel complete. Notice how the writer used a final sentence to summarize the paragraph below.

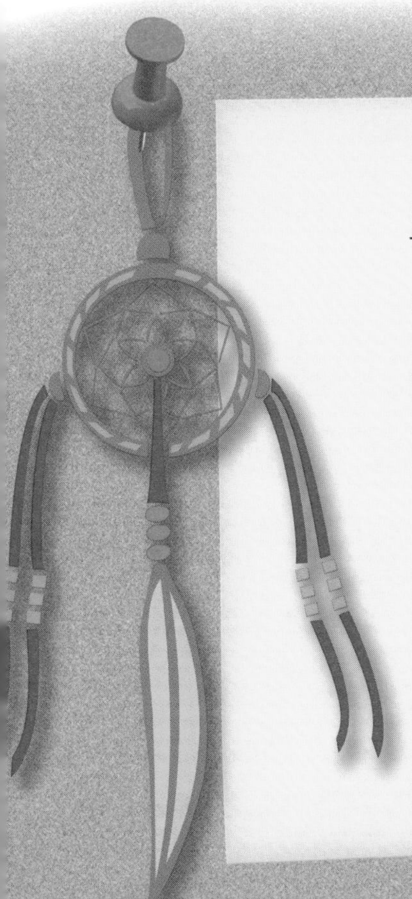

Children's museums today are not just filled with old objects to look at and read about. Children can play musical instruments at some museums. At others, they can build machines. Trying on clothes from other countries can carry children to a different place and time. Museums give kids of all ages a chance to imagine and explore. ← Closing sentence

TFK Tips for Writers

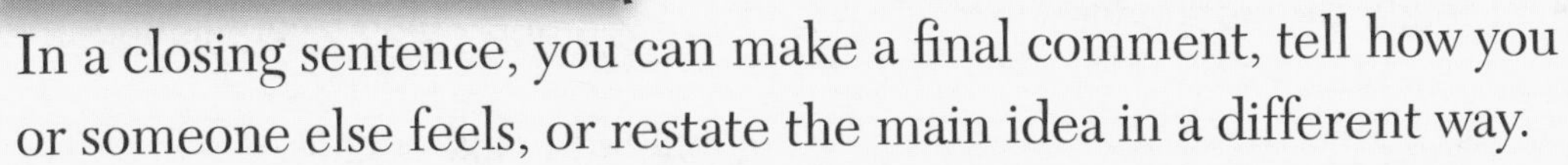

In a closing sentence, you can make a final comment, tell how you or someone else feels, or restate the main idea in a different way.

Using Capital Letters

Writers use capital letters to write proper nouns, the names of particular persons, places, or things. The chart below shows several other reasons why writers use capital letters.

for **names** of **people** and **places**	**Jim** and **Lisa** are my cousins from **California.**
for the **first word in a sentence**	**Two** polar bears played in the snow.
to write the pronoun ***I***	Yesterday **I** played soccer with my friends.
to name **days of the week, months,** and **holidays**	**Thanksgiving Day** is always on the fourth **Thursday** in **November.**
for **important words in a title**	***Green Eggs and Ham*** is a funny book.

Try This!

Read the sentences. Circle words that should begin with a capital letter.

1 My friend jeff lives in chicago.

2 we celebrate independence day in july.

3 greg read the book *half magic.*

4 Jason and i plan to go fishing in canada next august.

Choosing Punctuation

Writers use punctuation marks to show where a sentence ends. Look back at page 67 to review which punctuation marks to use for different kinds of sentences. The **comma** is another kind of punctuation. It tells a reader to pause briefly. Commas are used to separate words so that their meaning is clear. Here are some ways to use commas.

to separate three or more **words in a series**	Steve's favorite hobbies are drawing**,** reading**,** and playing baseball.
to separate the **month and day** from the **year**	My Uncle Frank got married in Chicago on June 28**,** 2003.
to separate the names of **a city and a state**	Last summer we spent our vacation in Orlando**,** Florida.

TFK Tips for Writers

Writers also use periods

- for **titles of people** written as abbreviations.
  Mr. and **Mrs.** Green visited **Dr.** Sharp.
  Note: The title **Ms** does not use a period.
- for **initials.**
  The letter was signed by Kathy **A.** Harris.

Time to Edit

Look at a paragraph, story, or report you have written. Check to be sure you have used capital letters and punctuation marks correctly.

Check Your Spelling

When you spell words correctly, others can easily read and understand what you write. Often it helps to compare a word you are trying to spell with other words that have the same sounds. Here are some patterns that will help you.

Sound and Letter Patterns

Long Vowel Sounds				
m**ai**l	h**e**	w**i**ld	s**o**	c**ue**
pl**ay**	d**ee**p	b**y**	l**oa**d	r**u**l**e**
t**a**k**e**	sp**ea**k	r**i**d**e**	n**o**t**e**	
n**ei**ghbor	funn**y**	n**igh**t	gr**ow**	

Other Vowel Sounds				
f**er**n	c**or**n	m**ar**k	f**ear**	h**ow**
f**ir**m	fl**oor**	h**ear**t	b**ear**	r**ou**nd
w**or**d	p**our**		l**ear**n	
t**ur**n	b**oar**d			

Try This!

Circle any words that are misspelled in the sentences below. Write the correct spelling above the word.

1 What did you lern from the book about bears?

2 As the stourm got closer, the wind started to bloa.

3 Jake fownd some shells on the beach.

More Sound and Letter Patterns

Beginning and Ending Consonant Blends				
trim	**sn**ap	**cl**ick	**fr**ee	be**st**

Words That Mean More Than One					
cat	bus	fox	dish	monk**ey**	penn**y**
cat**s**	bus**es**	fox**es**	dish**es**	monk**eys**	penn**ies**

Words with *ed* and *ing* Endings			
jump	play	smil**e**	pa**t**
jump**ed**	play**ed**	smil**ed**	pa**tt**ed
jump**ing**	play**ing**	smil**ing**	pa**tt**ing

Try This

Add an ending to make each word mean more than one.

class _____ box _____ hat _____ bush _____

Spell Syllables

Divide long words into syllables and sound out each part to help you spell the words correctly.

wil•low ti•ger in•sect
im•por•tant veg•e•ta•ble

Time to Edit

Read something you have written. Pay close attention to spelling. Circle any words you are unsure of. Check their spellings in the dictionary.

Using Proofreading Marks

Proofreading is like detective work. Writers learn to look carefully to find and correct mistakes in their writing. All writers use a special set of marks to show what changes need to be made.

Common Proofreading Marks

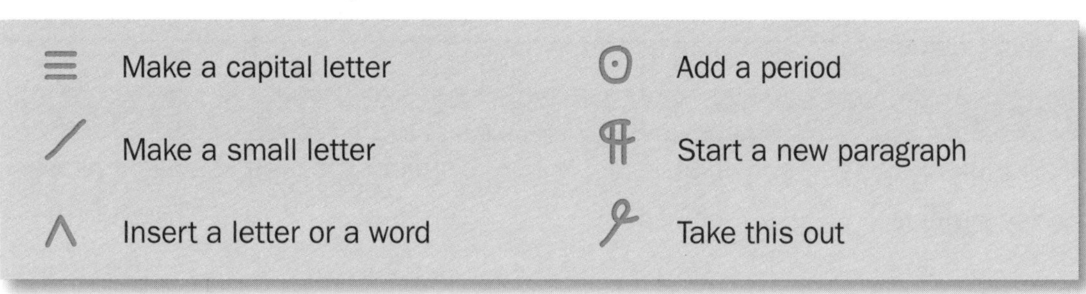

Mark	Meaning	Mark	Meaning
≡	Make a capital letter	⊙	Add a period
/	Make a small letter	¶	Start a new paragraph
∧	Insert a letter or a word	℘	Take this out

Try This!

Look at the proofreading marks in the paragraph below. What changes would you make?

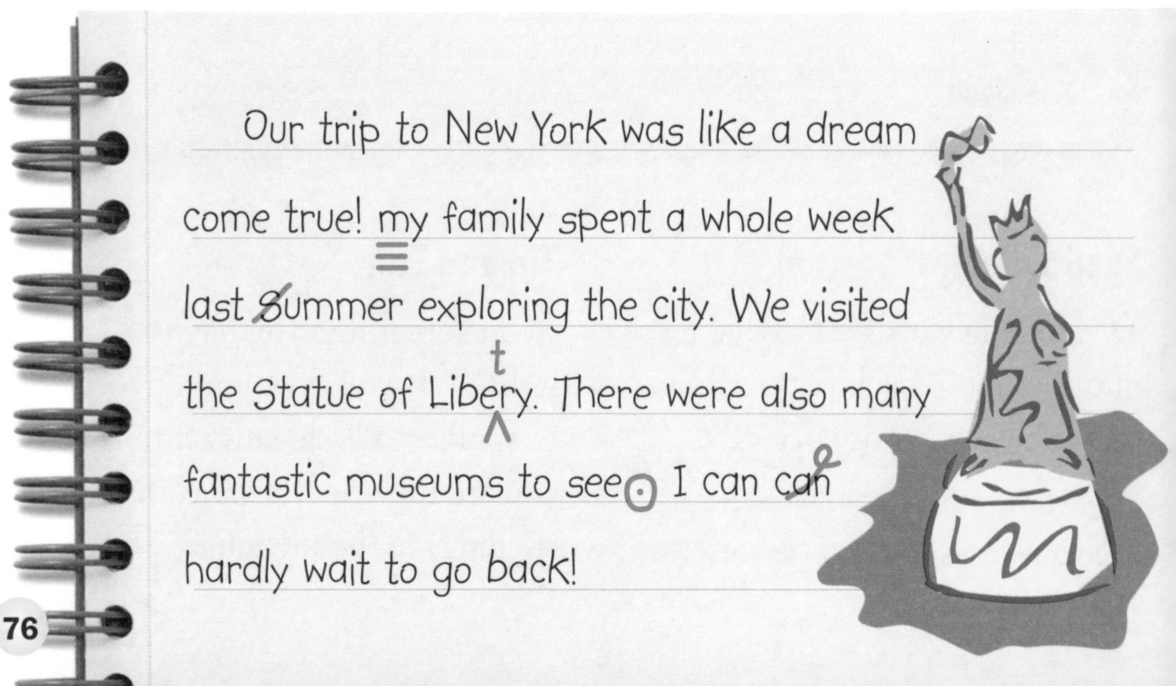

Tips for Proofreaders

Here are a few suggestions for finding and fixing mistakes in your writing.

Before you proofread, set your writing aside for a couple of hours. You will be more likely to catch mistakes if you take a break and return to your writing later with a fresh mind.

Read aloud what you have written. This is a great way to "hear" whether your writing makes sense.

Share your writing. Have a partner, friend, or family member read your work. Ask them to comment on things they like and things you might do better.

Time to Edit

The following paragraph is the opening for a story called "A Super Bowl for Kids!" Proofread the paragraph. Use proofreading marks to show mistakes that need to be fixed.

Rain pours out of the florida sky like a waterfall. Mike Boyle is as wet as a sponge. Mike plays quarterback for the Huskies of Plymouth, New Hampshire The Huskies are playing in a final gme at the Pop Warner national championships.

Try This!

Proofread the passage carefully. Use proofreading marks to show the mistakes you find.

On January 3, a spacecraft floo toward Mars at 12,000 miles per hour. Scientists at NASA had only one question: Would the craft land safely Then they got a a signal. "We see it!" cheered Wayne lee and others. The craft, called *Spirit,* had safely bounced onto mars.

Proofreader's Checklist

Here is a checklist you can use whenever you proofread.

- ☐ I wrote complete sentences.
- ☐ I indented all paragraphs.
- ☐ I used capital letters correctly.
- ☐ I checked my writing for errors in punctuation.
- ☐ I checked my writing for misspelled words.
- ☐ I made a neat final copy of my writing.

Time to Edit

Proofread something you have written. Use the checklist to help you find and mark any mistakes you have made. Make changes and write a final copy.

TFK Tips for Writers

Do you need to proofread even if you write with a computer? Yes! Computer spell-check programs catch some mistakes, but not all of them.

5
Publishing
Time to write your final copy and share it with others

Publishing Your Best

Good writers do not publish everything they write. They publish only their best writing. How do writers decide which piece or pieces are their best writing? Here are some questions you can ask to help you decide.

- Do I want to share this piece of writing with others? Why?
- Is my writing clear?
- Is my message clear?
- Does my piece of writing have a strong beginning and a strong ending?
- Is there any part I want to change before I publish it?
- Do I need pictures or graphs to make the presentation better?

TFK Tips for Writers

Publish writing that you like. Chances are that if you like a piece of writing, others will, too.

Ways to Publish Your Writing

The chart below shows a few different kinds of writing and different ways to publish them.

Kinds of Writing	Ways to Publish
Story such as a folktale, fairy tale, or adventure	• Add pictures to your story. • Make a Big Book. • Voice-record your story. • Put your story together with those of classmates to make a class book.
Personal narrative or biography	• Read aloud in an Author's Chair. • Dress up as the person you wrote about in your biography and tell your story to the class.
Report	• Make a booklet. • Add photos, maps, drawings, diagrams, or charts. • Make a poster to go with your report.
News story	• Put your news story with those of classmates to make a class newspaper or magazine. • Post your news stories as part of a school online newspaper.
Opinion essay, review, or editorial	• Make a comic strip. • Submit to a school or class newspaper. • Send as part of an email to friends or family.

Publishing on a Computer

You may decide to make your final copy and publish it on a computer. Use these tips to help you.

Create a Good Look

Design

Begin with a title page. Center the title and type your name below it. Then think about how you will arrange your writing on the rest of the pages. Include a mix of sentences and art to give your work a pleasing appearance.

Fonts

Using different fonts, or print styles, can add interest to your writing. Choose fonts that you like, but be sure they are easy to read. Italic and bold print are sometimes used to draw attention to special words or sentences. Here are some different fonts you might try.

Times
Times Italic
Helvetica
Helvetica Bold

Type Sizes

Choose a type size that makes your writing easy to read. A page filled with tiny print may be hard to read. Twelve-point type works well for most kinds of writing, such as stories and news reports. Use larger type and bold for titles and headlines. Compare these type sizes.

10-point type
12-point type
14-point type

Add Visuals

Art

Art adds interest to your writing. It can also help readers understand information you are presenting. There are different ways to include art with your writing.

- Use the computer's Paint or Draw features to create an original picture.
- Place computer clip art on the pages.
- Copy a photograph with a scanner. Then insert it electronically into the file.
- Leave space on the pages to draw or paste pictures after the pages have been printed.

Tables and Charts

Tables and charts give readers more information about your topic. They provide facts in a clear way that is easy to understand. For example, bar graphs can be useful for presenting the results of surveys and for showing facts about "how many."

Print, Save and File

Print

After you have made final corrections to your writing, print a final copy. You may choose paper with colors or special designs. Remember, though, that some colors can make your pages hard to read.

Save

You can save the file for each piece you have written on the computer in electronic folders. Saving files makes it easy for you to compare your writing with pieces you have written in the past. This will help you see the progress you are making.

File

You can organize your writing in separate folders. You might create a folder for each kind of writing, such as one for stories, one for reports, and so on. You might also make a folder for writing that you are still working on.

Vocabulary
Time to think
about the words
you use

Words to Write With

When you write, you need lots of words. When you are looking for just the right words, try some of these. You can add your own favorites to the words in each list, too. And, remember, words are to write with!

Frequently Used Words

1. about
2. always
3. because
4. does
5. father
6. house
7. mother
8. only
9. school
10. start

Time to Write

Make a list of words you use a lot in your writing.

1 ____________________

2 ____________________

3 ____________________

4 ____________________

Frequently Misspelled Words

1. always
2. again
3. believe
4. friend
5. let's
6. said
7. then
8. their
9. there
10. where

Time to Write

Check the spelling of words you often misspell. Then list them below.

1 ____________________

2 ____________________

3 ____________________

4 ____________________

Vivid Verbs

1. stir
2. creep
3. dart
4. race
5. prowl
6. rustle
7. giggle
8. tickle
9. twist
10. whisper

Time to Write

Make a list of vivid verbs you like. Try using them in your writing.

1 ______________________________ 3 ______________________________

2 ______________________________ 4 ______________________________

Contractions

1. doesn't (does not)
2. don't (do not)
3. he'll (he will)
4. she'll (she will)
5. they're (they are)
6. we're (we are)
7. won't (will not)
8. wouldn't (would not)
9. you'll (you will)
10. you're (you are)

Time to Write

Make a list of other contractions that you know.

1 ______________________________ 3 ______________________________

2 ______________________________ 4 ______________________________

Compound Words

1. airport
2. birthday
3. downstairs
4. football
5. homework
6. playground
7. rainbow
8. skateboard
9. toothbrush
10. weekend

Time to Write

Make a list of other compound words you know.

1 ______________________________

2 ______________________________

3 ______________________________

4 ______________________________

Commonly Confused Homonyms

1. nose
knows
2. wait
weight
3. son
sun
4. blue
blew
5. hear
here
6. one
won
7. see
sea
8. ate
eight
9. brake
break
10. meat
meet

Time to Write

Make a list of other pairs of homonyms. Learn to use each word correctly.

1 ______________________________

2 ______________________________

3 ______________________________

4 ______________________________

Citizenship and Community

1. city
2. cooperate
3. country
4. freedom
5. law
6. legal
7. mayor
8. neighborhood
9. volunteer
10. vote

Time to Write

Make a list of other words that will help you write about being a member of a community.

1 ______________________
2 ______________________
3 ______________________
4 ______________________

Feelings and Emotions

1. amazed
2. angry
3. calm
4. excited
5. joyful
6. lonely
7. patient
8. proud
9. scared
10. tired

Time to Write

Make a list of other words that name feelings. Try to use these words when you write.

1 ______________________
2 ______________________
3 ______________________
4 ______________________

More Words to Write With

Different kinds of writing call for special kinds of words. Look at the word lists on these pages. Can you think of a time when you might use these words?

Imagination and Adventure

1. action
2. castle
3. climb
4. dragon
5. explore
6. giant
7. hidden
8. knight
9. rescue
10. underwater

Time to Write

Make a list of other words that help readers use imagination. Include these words in fantasies and adventure stories you write.

1 ______________________________

2 ______________________________

3 ______________________________

4 ______________________________

Space and Technology

1. comet
2. computer
3. lunar
4. orbit
5. planets
6. remote
7. satellite
8. shooting star
9. telescope
10. universe

Time to Write

Make a list of other words about space and technology. Use them to add realistic details to your stories and reports.

1 ______________________________

2 ______________________________

3 ______________________________

4 ______________________________

Holidays

1. New Year's Day
2. Martin Luther King, Jr. Day
3. Valentine's Day
4. Memorial Day
5. Independence Day
6. Labor Day
7. Halloween
8. Veterans Day
9. Thanksgiving Day
10. Hanukkah
11. Christmas
12. Kwanzaa

Time to Write

Make a list of other holidays that you celebrate with family members and friends.

1 ______________________________

2 ______________________________

3 ______________________________

4 ______________________________

Transportation and Geography

1. airplane
2. beach
3. bicycle
4. continent
5. country
6. desert
7. island
8. mountain
9. ocean
10. train

Time to Write

Make a list of other words about geography and travel. Look at this list when you describe the setting in a story.

1 ______________________________

2 ______________________________

3 ______________________________

4 ______________________________

Index

G

H

I

L

M

N

O

Stone Soup
Hansel and Gretel

Traits of Good Writing Index